ANOINTING PRAISE IN POETRY

ANOINTING PRAISE IN POETRY

Peggy S. McDougald

authorHOUSE®

AuthorHouse™ LLC
1663 Liberty Drive
Bloomington, IN 47403
www.authorhouse.com
Phone: 1-800-839-8640

Published by AuthorHouse 01/08/2014

ISBN: 978-1-4918-3806-8 (sc)
ISBN: 978-1-4918-3805-1 (e)

Library of Congress Control Number: 2013921573

Contents

The essence of this book is faith. Faith begins with believing and faith is realized in conquering ones foe. With faith one can overcome obstacles that would otherwise defeat. Faith makes the weak powerful and turns mountains into foothills. There is an unconquerable spirit in men and women when they believe. To my grandmother my Native American Queen who made me believe that the im in impossible was a misprint. To my mother who is a realist. With these two and God I cannot fail. These are poems, sayings and stories of survival and being more than you were before. Some are unbelievable if you lack faith. The spirit of your mind and soul must be one. When they come together you can achieve what once was impossible. Your journey toward faith begins with a thought, a word, knowing and finally an accomplishment. It is my desire that in this book you find a joyous celebration of all that you can be. Please share the spiritual faith that exists within each of us.

I Live

There are times for us each day. That time is riddled with moments preceded and followed by seconds and moments. And there is a time when they culminate as one. In these moments I am given joy, arrays of peace and happiness. And within the times of those moments I live. I ride the tides of oceans of blues, greens and gray foam. I float among clouds of bright colors they are propelled by the breeze of winds small and mighty. I fly with the birds. I skate down the heights of mountains and I fall into valleys of colors. The floral plants, flowers and grasses speak to me. The creatures of the Master bid me hello and farewell.

And then just for the thrill I ride with the tortoise and lizard into a land where no water is seen. Here in this place I spread myself out and lay upon its sands. The heat of its loss is felt within all that live In the place of none. But this place has secrets of life for the ones who would only quietly stop and gives it ear. I hear the words. I rise up with a gleeful laugh. I pull it cactus and it gives pain and bloodies my fingers. But I smile as my lips and tongue taste it nectar and gives unto my body living moisture. The entire world speaks to me. In my moments of time strung together by seconds and moments before and after, I live.

Settling

Who am I? I am my best. Who am I? I am one who will not settle for less. If that make me the one you fear and want to be. You can deceive others but it is not so easy deceiving self. I am the knight who storms the castle and wins beyond all odds. There inside the castle were problems that needed to be solved. So I did what needed to be done. I am Joan of Arc giving and dying for the belief that I hold inside my soul. I know my fate and my end but I must help the ones who will without cause take my life.

I am like a sand bag that absorbs the waters that hold back the floods of destruction. I am like a vaccine made to save the masses. I am like a storm cloud that brings the rain. Who am I? I am the giver of the horn of life. I am you, the one that you pretend to be when a pretty girl or a handsome young man passes by. I am what you want to be. I am food; I am a meal that nourishes a hungry soul. I am me. I am his ever growing and improving child. Then I am you; you are me wanting, needing but never settling for less.

Plans for My Eternal Home

It is a place beyond this life that has been offered and it awaits me.

It is a where I desire to go when my task and labors here are done.

This place is not now within human sight for my spirit is earth bound.

But I know it will not always be this way. I know it is there and I will go.

This oasis in which I wish to reside is known as my eternal heavenly home.

In this place my soul shall at last receive its rest. I am claiming an eternal rest.

There are requirements that must be met for your and my entrance there.

One is holding on to my faith. With it I can endure all and claim my crown.

The other is believing; belief will help me return to the path if I should stray.

All the sins of this world I will survive. I am his but he allows me to choose my fate.

And it is Him I will follow. A place by his side or at his feet is

better than a
nanosecond in hell. I
will not be among the
souls who denied
him and forfeited
heaven and all its
glory.

This place of wondrous
joys is where my soul
has plans to reside for
all of eternity. On this
place I will continuously
stamp my name. A
home of heavenly
treasures my soul has
sought and placed its
claim. I will seek nor
accept no other's
place. I know what the
Savior has and what he
ask of me. He ask that
I do his work and give
my best and nothing
less. He'll not ask me
what Mary, Tony or
Paul did. My salvation
is about me and what
I've done.

Worldly Child

If you want to be a worldly child, there is
nothing much to do. Turn yourself over to the
devil, and he will make use of you. He will
offer pearls of dust and gold that rusts. If you
just don't love yourself, and you want nothing
good for you, give yourself to the devil and do
as he says. It is all up to you. Is this the life
you want for yourself? If your soul is for sale,
the devil wants one like you.

It was your soul and your choice. You gave it
away, so no sad cries for you. Should you
decide that you are better than the plans that
the devil has for you, in the Bible there is a
remedy for all the Devil has for you. There is
One who has stood up and died for you. He is
just a whisper away. Struggles though tough
are like spit in the ocean with God on your
side. Do this. Call God!

Grace

If I had to choose one of the many gifts God
gave to us, I would chose grace. Grace is
what sustains us. It energizes us; it gives us a
purpose and reason. Because I have grace,

he will keep me. He will calm my turbulent waters. For I belong to God whatever the season. I can tell the world I am here and God gave me grace. But above it all I thank God, for he did not make me choose. He gave it all for me.

Pray

Each time I pray it is a letter to my God. Sometimes I thank him, and there is always praise for what he has done. Also, I give praise for the things he did not give. I've prayed for things not needed. I've prayed for events that would have created wrong in my life. As I learn, I pray that his will be done. I am thankful and blessed for what he give to us daily.

As he grants my prayers by what he gives to me, he also answers them by the things he keeps from me. He kept the car. I knew it was not for me, but the human asked anyway. He blessed me by fulfilling my needs, and there

were times he blessed me just because. Even
when I did not ask, he knew my needs and he
gave it anyway.

Daughter of Mine

You are my conscience, my yardstick toward perfection.
When I think I have reached my highest, you give more.
You are loved for the awe-inspiring woman that you are.
I am proud to call you my daughter; no mother got more.
Thank you for your good, you have made me proud.
I will love you beyond forever. I am your champion!
Your mom

You were born

The day you were born was the day God gave me a glimpse of
an angel. Although you are not perfect, you always give your
best. You are a wonder to behold. When there is a task to be
done, you are on it. You are a joy, not only to me, but to all who
know you. If not, then something is wrong with them. To my
darling ones, the joy of my life, I love you.

I Touched Him

I touched my Jesus, and he completed me. With one single touch, he filled my unclean soul. Never will I be as I was after the touch that Jesus gave. It answers a question that Jesus is indeed real. There is no other who could or would have done what he has done for me.

He Loves Me

I am ripped, torn, and ragged with jagged edges. They say I have no class, culture, or beauty. They say I am just rambling along on life's highway. I know I am not perfect; nevertheless, God looked and saw my worth. To him I am a precious being. God, in his wisdom, loves me.

She Loved Us

All my life you have showed me that you cared. When I was a precocious little child I knew you loved me still. Through the years, you taught me, guided me, and made me what I am today. Who could ask more of another than what you gave to me? I love you with all I am, with all my heart I will remember. The love and respect you gave and taught will be carried by us all. We'll love you forever.

God and Man

A man without a dream is a man left afloat.
A dream without vision is lost upon the tides.
A man must stand and run even without legs.
A man who seeks a goal must first make a plan.
Planning for dreams is a deed of accomplishment.
These things can only come true for God and man.

Forever Praise

Should I have limbs that labored not, and did not function, I'd
praise.
If I had no limbs, hands, or feet, I would praise the Lord with my
spirit.
If my eyes no sight, my ears no hearing, my mouth no speech,
I'd praise.
No matter the condition, I would give the highest praise to God
for my Soul.

The Power of Faith

Faith is the hand that calms a raging sea. It is the love that spares a life in the middle of a torrent ocean. Faith goes beyond all knowledge of science, mechanics, or any mortal understanding that we may have. Faith is things heard and unheard; it is the seen and unseen. It is a joy that surpasses all its possibilities and any what ifs or tries of man.

Faith is the knowing that without an inkling of doubt that what God has will work when all human deeds have failed. Faith has no reservations or uncertainties. Faith never compromises or falls short of a miracle. Though it may not be the miracle we expect at the time we expect but it comes. Faith supersedes the believing and arrives at fait accomplice.

God's Work in Progress

I'm God's work in progress. Look at what he has done with me. He has made me walk upright. That's what he has done with me. God has shown me the beauty of his world that my eyes had not seen.

He taught me to love and give to others, as he has given unto me. He has shown me the difference between man's right and God's.

Nobody but God

There is no one like my God. He is with me now and always.
He walks with me both night and day, never leaving me alone.
He guides me through my troubled times and into the sunlight.
I rejoice in the good and bad, for He always walks with me still.
When I could not walk, he carried me. He has great love for all.
Who could have done this with so much care? Nobody; only my
God.

The Shining Light

I know a light that is greater and brighter than any star.
God the Father is the light whom I have chosen to serve.
Father, I ask may I serve and be with you throughout eternity.

God, for me there can be no one more wonderful than you.
You gave to your children the earth and heavens for us all.
Even though we failed, you give us chances at redemption.
Father, I give myself to you; I am here to serve and praise.
Lord, I ask that you let your light shine within and upon me.
I will own the light and share it, and allow it to shine from
within.

The Fight

Happiness, joy, and peace are the most lofty of dreams for a
man, woman, or child.
A seat in the kingdom is greater; it is not a dream but a gift to
those who serve God.
This gift will be given to those who have the faith and the
endurance to finish the fight.

Looking Forward to the Day

Every time I see awesomeness of my world, I see God, and I look
forward to the day.
It is impossible to see and not marvel at the miracles of life
and all that he has made.

There are no words that could describe or express the visions
my eyes and heart behold.
It is an adventure to behold all the glory and wonders of my
Father, so I go forward to my day.

A Well-Fed Soul

My soul is filled with all it needs.
Jesus feeds it each and every day.
I thank Him for feeding my old soul.
He gave me light, as I was in the dark.
When I gave Him hate, He gave me love.
When I wallowed in evil, He tamed the sin.
He taught me caring in an unforgiving world.
The Father loved me, so I could return His love.
My Father prepared my soul and filled its needs.

He Is

I hear the waters rolling against the shores; they seem to say
his name.

The whooshing wind through the leaves, I hear the wonder of his
words.

The grass sways to and fro, as if to sing the praises of his
glorious love.

All the things that he has made stand and give tribute unto
him, our Father.

Thanks to our God, the maker of all things in the heavens and
upon the earth.

We know that he cares for all his creations, but to man he gives
much affection.

He gave his beloved son so that we, his children, could live here and ever after.

What a magnificent, loving God! We are all the recipients of a love with no equal.

Seeing Miracles in Prayer

There is a sight beyond the eyes. It is a sight that only a soul can see. It is a sight that can see within the dimmest of light. It is the sight of the Father. With this sight the smallest and biggest of miracles can be seen. This is the sight that envisions its prayer becoming more in God hands.

It is a sight that knows the moment a prayer changes and becomes a miracle. Seeing a miracle in a prayer is not for the faithless or weak of heart. It is for the men and women who give and bring honor to the Father. Would you join us in this family? It is the family of our Father is in heaven.

Offerings to the Soul

They work hard to kill the one inside. They do it, not with deeds, but with words said to mind and the soul. They offer what the mind and soul has no need of.

"Who are they?" you ask. "I know them." Do you? They are envy, lust, greed, and desires of man and the Devil's mind. Be no fool and say they do not exist.

You meet them on the streets most every day. They look back at you from a storefront. While you are riding down the road, looking into a car's reflection, they're there. They are looking through the eyes of you.

Living my Life

Some say, "Live not in the past; live for the moments in the time of now."
For me, I will live in the future, the present, and the past of all my days.
Life was given so we could do so; it cannot be just moments in the now.

With each ounce of life, I will live now; it is a presentation for our future.
My life will be as the waters of an ocean; I'll lap it dry with a thirst of living.
Each moment will be recorded as a book of mind, to be proof of my deeds.

The lessons for me will be the living I give to others I encounter daily. When I depart this world; I want life to say these things of me: "She lived for the coming.
She gave to and loved living. She shared the moment and let it be said; "she fully lived."

The One

When I found him, my friends said, "Girl, he's the one." I thought so too. He is the one. I felt him in my soul. I was excited that he lived on high and that he walked really tall. But it had nothing to do with his height or where he did reside. This is it; he is the one I have waited for. If I wish, he will be with me always. Because of him I shall never be alone. When I call, he hears. He is the one I want eternity with. He is the one worthy, and I cannot give enough. I will serve him through my work for and with his children. Yes, he is my heavenly Father. He is the one who has the power to save me and gave a future to a grateful soul.

Making a Better Me

He gave to me the power to be a better me. I look inside to see the power of me. He gave the gift to make a better and richer me. My spirit was faded, and dull. It could hardly be seen; to God, what an awful sight I must have been.

He helped me. He knew there was work to be done. Together with God, the Father's help I will build my crown. For He has given me all I need to make a better me.

Words of Wisdom

Saying I:
When one is looking for the light they must travel through the dark.

Saying II:
There are those who feel safe on earth because they believe that the devil resides in hell. That is his home but he has accumulated an inordinate amount of frequent flyer miles. So my friend this thought is foolish and requires reevaluation.

Saying III:
In my house there are a few rooms. But in the Father's heaven there are an unnamed amount of mansions. He has gone forth to prepare places for all his saved ones.

Saying IV:
A soul who works against its good loses itself a home in the kingdom.

Saying V:

Be not afraid, for the Father abides with us; he shall not leave or forsake his children (Deuteronomy 32:6).

Did He Cry?

Did Jesus cry when he looked upon us and there was no answer? Tell me, Father, tell me was he sad though he knew what fools we were? We know he traded his life in return for ours heavenly one. Angels, did you cry for God's only son? Did you? When we, the sheep, nailed down The Father's Son? Angels, where there cries for the sacrifice that was his only child?

Among his earthly children was there a tear of shame when we crucified the Father's Son?

What did he think of us when the deed was done? What a gracious and giving God he is. Did God turn his head when it was done? Though he knew his son would rise again. Was there mourning among the Angels when Jesus suffered in pain? What a price to pay for a deed that was a must and had to be done. Oh, what a love he has for us.

He Was All I Had

I had a mother and father. I have sisters and brothers. But when taking my divine finals, I found I had no one. My mother, my father, my sisters, nor my brothers could go there with me. My afterlife was a journey for one and that one was me. The travel plans were made for one just me alone. No family or friends could go on this trip we each must make. It is required we make it on our own or at least with no mortal being. And there I found the Father and Angels were there. I found that there was no need for any other. I was indeed blessed, for all I had was all I need of. As always my Father was there lighting the way for me.

I Responded Not

He spoke to me, and I answered not. He called my name, and to him no answer came. He looked down and saw my plight. He said, "I am your father, and you are my child. Why do you not call to me?" I was ashamed, so still I answered not. I allowed the human in me to call the shots in my life. What a fool I'd been. Would I be foolish still? If he called again, would I answer? Would I be still the fool and call nor answer not? I couldn't wait. I made my choice. I will call to him. Where should a child be except with a parent who gives love and caring?

The Inner World and Me

All my needs were provided for by the world in which I lived. In this place there maybe; there could be one, a few or many. We must leave this world of mine, made for one, two, or a few These few months are a lifetime for me, the few or for us all. Still in the world things revolve around me or one, two, or a few. In this world it takes just nine short months for a life to grow. But for me the one and the two, or there may be few. It is a lifetime.

Jesus Is

Jesus is the heart of me; he is the soul of me.
No matter where I am, in my coming and going,
He is there, if I have need of more: he is all to me.
I will allow no other, for I would not be his child.

Despite the things I did, he never left me alone.
The Father has always been my heart and soul.
Even when I refused to admit that he was there.
Jesus you gave love to a wretched one as was I.

I Heard

Walking in the desert deep, I heard of the name of Jesus and
his mightiness. On the floor of a valley with no name, I heard
his call and the splendor in the words spoken by the earth.
Standing on a mountaintop I could see the world above, and
below I heard his name still.

I heard him on the clear blue sea, I heard him in the storm.
Everywhere I went his voice called out to me. Sitting on a city
bus I decided to stop and answer the call. I said, "Jesus, I give
you my all." From this day forth when I heard the word of God, I
listened and obeyed.

Speak, and I Hear

Lord, speak to me, because I need your guidance today. I do not
know how to live without your loving care. Lord, will you speak so
that I may hear? Father, speak to me and tell me what I must
do. Lord, when I hear the words within my spirit I will listen to
your voice and follow what you ask of me. And, Father, I will
praise you all the more when you speak and I hear your words.

How Could I?

How could I give less when God gave me his best?
I can give to or do for others, as the He has given me.
How could I do less when Jesus gave me his life?
I'll give him all so I may be known as one of his own.

The Crowd

I went to church last Sunday and sat among the crowd that
were all my friends in God. Together we praised and blessed
his holy name. The singing was a great thrill for us all. On this
we were one. Though we all gave to Him in ways so differently,

it was a sight to behold. Some sprang to their feet at the word; others sat down and relished inside with the joy of it. An uplifting time of gladness was had by us all; the old and young alike. We felt quite different as we left this place of praise. Though we were pleased with our actions this day; the question is! What did the Father think of the praise we gave this day and every day?

Everywhere

As I drove down my street I observed the people, and the look upon their faces was joy. In the elevator it was there stamped upon the people's smiling faces. On the way to the stores, amid the throng of wanderers, I perceived a caring love encased deep within their hearts. What had happened to my fellow men and women to make them behave in such a manner? Where was the discord I tried to avoid and held in distain on the days that had passed?

I stepped in my door at home. There it was in the sounds of my family's laughter. What was happening? Was there some special event or holiday I had forgotten or missed? This was not my life of yesterdays. Thankfully, I had found the Savior; now I knew his love was real. The difference was me. How I saw the world was coming from within me.

Leaning

There was a friend whose burdens were very heavy indeed. So he leaned on a friend to make the burden lighter. Grateful for the lighter load, he allowed a friend to lean on him. Then another leaned on. She, in turn, allowed another to join the line and give comfort to another. Some burdens were heavy and others not so much. But a burden is a burden, and help is sometimes required. The line grew long. And soon with time it was longer still. With so many burdens heavy and small, it looked as if there was nor would there be any relief in sight. As each in turn leaned, some turned and looked at the others. Then there were others who began to sigh. Many wondered if and when the loaded burdens would cause them all to fall. But still there were additions to the leaning line. Then a voice was heard by those who chose to listen. It clearly said "I am the beginning and the end, I am here, so none who believe in me may fall."

Show Me Faithfulness

I say to myself, "I will be faithful in all I do. When I fail, I will not give excuses or reasons why." Faithful is a word that can and should cover all aspects of our lives. Yet still I give excuses. I say, "I forgot," "The baby was sick," or "A friend needed help." The most passé excuse is "My car didn't start." Let's not forget I can also blame the traffic. It was such a major event. There are excuses and trouble to use that occur most every day.

Then my soul says to myself, "Show me your faithfulness".
These and others I used as personal excuses for failure. Truth
is truth and today I failed because I did not try. Trying took too
long, so I accepted the failure. There is an excuse.' I cried. There
was just not time to do it all. Now I know when I fail I must
accept that it is not the other things in my life. I fail because I
did not show the faithfulness to God that he gives to me.

After

After the storms of life, how can you start over again?
I ask of myself. Did I learn what he taught from the storm?
After the storm, how do you learn to make a better you?
Did I understand the meaning of me and all God's worth?
Lord, you gave your promise. I have faith in all you've done.
You carried me. You will be there during and after my storm.

A Selfish Heart

I kept looking for possessions I thought I must have. My
friends had these things and so did people I cared little for.
They say to me, "God will provide your needs." My mind says "I

need things? My clothes are much too old. I've had my shoes for months on end. The furnishings in my home could use an update. The kids have had no new coats. Last year's clothing will never do. Mom is too old and sick to work. I would put her in a nursing home, but the people would take our money. How could I send her there and pay for the home they gave to me? So maybe if we ask God to help, he will answer my pray. He gave these things to them, so why would he not give it to me? They cannot be more deserving than me. Then my child looks at me with loving eyes. She says to me, 'I love you, grandma and everyone in the whole world. But grandma says God love us more. In her words I heard my mother's words but that is a lesson I will think on tomorrow.

Falling in Love Today

I fall in love most every
day. Each day it
changes.
I open my eyes, and the
world is somehow more.
Falling in love with God is
what I am made to do.
The weather or
circumstances cannot
control my lot.

Peggy S. McDougald

I am one not ruled by the
spin of a dime or turn of
tides.

The clouds may be dark
or sunny; still I fell in love
today.
Snow, hail, rain, or
thunderstorms may come
or they may not.
Days, sad or dreary can't
stop me, for today again I
fell in love.
All men are his, and God
in his wisdom gives us
love each day.
I choose to take his love
inside, tend it and share
what he gives.

The world's sadness
could not hold me down,
for again I fell in love.
Things not seen before
are for my eyes today; it
has been made anew.
What we did not feel on
yesterday is fresh, it is
untouched just for me.
Someone died and joined

the saints; a child was
born to this world of ours.
All these occurrences are
our life, and this all
renders it a day made of
love.

A Shining Spirit

He was sent into this world. He entered quietly and without
display. His spirit was ahead of man and time. His thoughts
and actions were above the rest. Before we thought the words
the melody and the music had left his mouth. And the music
was a joy to behold. He was ours, and we were his. We saw his
difference and rejoiced in it. Some were excited because of his
worth. Some were proud. Others were jealous. There were those
who sought his deadly demise. It caused pain and although it
was sad, it was a part of the master plan.

Some saw, heard and began to spread the word of his higher
calling. He healed the sick and raised the dead. Still none knew
the plans for his deathly end. Known by many names he was
sent by the Master. His mission was that he came to save
the world. His final end would make for us a life of ever after.
He knew of our needs and answered our prayers. The world had

a monumental need. It has need of more lights to shine. He taught us of our brighter light. He gave a promise of greater miracles if we would only believe. Do you choose to be and feel the love of it all?

I Forgot to Pray

Today I awoke with thoughts of granny and her prayers for me. I've bought a new car. I have the home of my dreams. I have money in the bank and a job that I love. My plans for my life are on track. Unlike others I passed on the way. I thought to myself, *Life has been good to me.* Then I heard her say "what a fool you are. "Child it was God". He was the One who brought you from there to here".

Father, I ask your forgiveness. I did not thank you for any of the things you've done. You loved and provided for me. Yet I gave you no praise. I did not give the love and understanding to others you gave to me along the way. I knew you walk with me. But, I cared only for self. Today I give thanks for those in my life who prayed when I forgot to pray. Forgive me Father; never again will I forget to pray.

Great Things

He has shown great things for me further down the road. But there in my face is that smiling devil. He has a sign that says, "Do not trespass. This path is not for you." This road has rocks; they are too heavy for you to carry. Come with me. There is an easier way. I say, "Devil, you cannot deceive me. My God goes down this road with me."

The devil pulled out a shiny object from his bag of tricks. He placed it upon his arm and artfully displayed the rarest of jewels. This possession that the devil held out to me was ever so inviting. I didn't think it would hurt to look. It was such a prize the devil had for me. But I knew the price; it was one my soul could not pay.

Happily I headed down the road to find what God had there for me. But, alas the devil was not through with me. "Are you having fun?" he asked. "Sure. The road that God has sent me down is not so rough. So be gone, Devil. I have no time for you." I had spoken to soon, for there were troubles I did not know on the path where I walked.

The Devil laughed from the other side; as I struggled to make my way through. The devil had his eyes on me to see just what I would do. So I sat down on the path that I traveled, and I prayed. I knew that there was someone to help. I had one inside, who, if he desired, could send someone or come himself and carry me.

I walk down the road on which God has sent me. I know the path may sometimes be difficult, but it is worth the toll. I have a burning need to join him in the kingdom. There is a cross that I must bear to enter his home. No matter what the devil does, there is a gift God gave to me. Put God in front, say "Devil, God has great things so be on your way."

Why?

I did wrong and broke a finger. It rightly hurt, but I asked, "Why me?"
The man I loved should have belonged to me, but I asked "Why me?"
I wanted it. It was mine, but another got it. I asked the Father, "Why me?"
I never cared if I should not possess it all, but I asked the Father, "Why me?"

They were all my desires, and I got them not, but I asked the Father, "Why me?"
I looked far and wide. Everyone's needs were met, and to him I asked, "Why me?"
The heavens opened up for me, and I saw that not everyone had all they wanted.
What a sucker I was. I had all my needs and many wants. Now, Lord, why me?

A Being

I gazed upon the ocean and saw its colors in unending glorious splendor. The water lapped, sometimes gently and at other times like a raging wind. The sands met it and sparkled, as if to say hello. When the sun rose it gave to the ocean a tender caress. And as I hold this sight within my vision, I am just a being.

I behold the splendor of the mountains high above me. They are dotted with trees of green, gold, and shades of colors in between. We know they live and are glad for it. They seem to say, "Come, look at the wonder of all he has made." And as I hold this sight within my vision I shout I am just a being.

I see his clouds while flying on a plane made by the genius of man. I pass by the clouds, or do they pass by me? They are painted with impressive colors that can never be duplicated by man, though he tries. I think if only I could touch, just a feel. And as I hold this sight within my vision, I am just a being.

Today, in the mirror I looked. I frowned and scoffed at the person I saw. I began to smile and laugh. Like all he made, he made many facets of me. He made me in his image and breathed into me a life. Within me he placed a soul. I am his; he is mine. He loves and cares for me. To God, the Father, I am more. I am his Being.

The Walk

I began my daily walk about town that had been gently forced upon me.

There beside the store stood people gazing upon some sight.

They were in awe over some unusual spectacle they observed.

I tried to turn the other way, but my curious mind would not allow it.

Some spoke of the beauty of God's work; others spoke of Mother Nature.

So I placed myself at the front of the crowd to see what they had seen.

My eyes did not see the things they had seen; I just saw an old stand.

They spoke of flowers and magnificent colors; this my eyes did not see.

I continued along this daily walk that was ever so gently forced upon me.

Where was the beauty of which they spoke? And where was this wonderful display?

Through my eyes I saw no beauty. I saw an old stand and ugliness.

So I turned and walked away from this. For me the view
provided no delight.

I continued along this daily walk that was ever so gently forced
upon me,

Entering a park where I once played. I heard birds chirping as
they sang melodies.

Butterflies danced happily along with sublime abandonment
from plant to plant.

The trees swayed in a welcoming hello. The squirrels were in a
foolish game of fuss and folly.

On this day the world seemed to be in harmony; but my heart
was in no mood for such elation.

In my heart was a crack that could not be mended, and it had
no desire to partake.

The freshness and joy of these simple things made me feel as if
I should bellow and scream.

I sat down on an old park bench. I held my head and closed my
eyes, for I could not see.

Looking up I saw an old friend, and I called to her; though she
was sick and frail still she smiled.

So I sat up tall and felt the joy that the day offered. I was glad
for the walk was not forced upon me.

Final Destination

As I leave this world and say my final good-byes, I pray I will see the ones who came to see me off. Children of mine and others who came take care. This will be my last journey, and I have planned to make its destination my greatest. I have read the book and did what was asked of me. I tried to follow his rules and listen to all that I had heard. I know that some will shed tears. It's okay; I have done the same for those I have known. I do this knowing I've done my best.

My children know that I will love you forever and some. God gave you to me, and I dedicated you to him. I have always known that I would need him to walk with us all. My darlings, I try not to be prideful, but you are the best of me that I have to give the world. In you God gave me one task: to raise the noblest human beings possible. This could only happen if I would follow his word and his teachings. Hearts of my heart, you have been the pride and joy of my life.

The gift of you was most precious and most appreciated. You have been my light when there was darkness. Jesus knew I needed you maybe more than you needed me. You have made me want to be a better me. There is one message I have given to you that can never be said enough. Hold tight to your faith. It will take you through the good and bad. With your faith you can climb mountains that you never knew existed. Life's destinations have many roads. Thankfully Heaven has one.

He Chose Me

When you look at yourself, what do you see? I chose God, and he saved me. I said, "Father," and he replied "yes, my child." I asked, "Father, may I walk with you?" He said, "I am here". So. I chose the Father. In spite of my past he gave his love. Or did he give me love because he knew I needed him so. I am so glad I chose Him. The real glory is that the Father chose me.

On a Trip with God

In the days of yond, I was maybe nine or ten. I lay under a mulberry tree, wondering what I could do. The world is such a boring place when you are nine or ten. In my life there were trees and more trees; it was all we could see. As I gazed into the sky I had thoughts of the places I wished to see. Then without any effort at all, my soul all on its own did take flight. I flew among the clouds, where I had never been before. A child's smile fell upon my face. I was delighted about the journey that I had been chosen to take. I had no thoughts of fear when we visited the city of Bethlehem. The alleys were cramped and small. But that mattered not to God and me, for we were in his sky and he was its Master.

I was flying with the Savior. What more was there to say? I glimpsed the place of his birth, or maybe it was just a dream. Then on to Egypt we went. There I saw many sights of which I had only dreamed. The pyramids they were brand-new. Into a cavern we flew and before I knew it years were gone. In a sliver of time and ages of years thieves had stolen the pharaoh's loot. How then would he buy his way to his heavenly home? Beside me I saw God shake his mighty head. Pharaoh needed no riches. Riches would not do, for they could never buy a heavenly home. Is the story true? Maybe the answer is yes or maybe no. But where else could a child of nine or ten have such a visit except on a trip with the Master; her Father?

My Last Day

I was pulled from my slumber by the sound of music in my head. *Late!* I ran for the bathroom, rushing through my shower. As I put on my clothes I heard a voice call to me again. I was busy, so I chose to ignore the call. There was no way. I did not have time. There were things at work that only I could do.

I had a working lunch, and it was good indeed. I got a client. It was great. I'd made money for us all. At one o'clock in the evening I heard the ringing of the bells. In it was a question for me. *Late?* The day was young; there were hours yet to go. "When I have time I will listen and deal with what you ask of me."

Then there was dinner, a meeting with friends, and a beer
or two. Driving home, I said to myself, "What a good day. I
accomplished much." Tomorrow there would also be much to do.
My plate would be filled with this and some of that. I entered
my home, and I turned off the alarm and turned on the tube.

There was a man talking about God and Jesus being one and
the same. I was tired. I sat down to listen. But the soothing
voice had my head nodding, and my body wished for sleep.
My evening tasks finished none left undone. "Not now!" I still
ignored the voice. Tomorrow was another day, and I would still
have much to do.
Today I woke with an empty mind. I lay on my bed feeling sad
and alone. The hands on the clock read 6:00 a.m.
But there was no music pulling me from my slumber. *I am in my
prime. This cannot be me.* Gone was the voice

A Meeting

Last night I dreamed the Father was giving me an audience I
had so long sought.
I had made a special request to him, and he had sent his
answer in a dream for me.

This audience needed no physical death, sad passing, or meetings on the other side.

For the meeting with him, I rose early from my bed. I had questions. I would not be late.
I searched through my closet and dressers; I was looking for the perfect outfit to wear.
I had a meeting with my heavenly Father. For him I wanted to be and look my best.

I placed my favorite hat upon my head. You know the one that make my cheeks and eyes smile.
My questions I needed to ask were ready; I had placed them within the pages of my Bible.
For my meeting with the Father I had planned all that I would say; I had years to rehearse.

We were in the car, my thoughts and I, as I headed to the church. Then there came the shame.
I held my Bible to my chest; the answers were there, but I had not heard. Oh, God what am I?
God had spoken to me, but I had not listened. There were answers in my Bible, but I had not read.

A Father

A father is such a
gift that all would
wish for one.
A father is more
than one who gives
or has a seed.
Fathers are such a
gift that they are
very hard to find.
A father is more
than one who
resides in the home.
He is the one who
will take time to
nourish a child.

A father is such a
gift that he is prized
above all things.
A father is more
than jewels, gold, or
precious metals. A
father is surely a
perfect gift that God
offers to men.
Fathers are the
ones who cleans a
nose or soothes a

cry at night. He is a
man who receives
what God has given
with joy.

A father does not
come in seasons,
for he is a father in
his heart. A man is
a father not only
because he gives
the seed of his
loins. A man is a
father when he
loves and fosters a
child that's in need.
Would you give and
be a father to one
who has no father at
all? Fathers who
look the other way,
tell me, are you
human at all?

Looking for the Savior

I was walking through this world and looking down its dusty
roads. I decided I should seek the Savior and make him mine.
I was sure it would be a daunting task. Therefore, I must
immediately be on my way.

I plotted my course straight ahead so that him I would find.
I dared not look left or right. What should I see but a woman
I knew, standing on the side? I saw the tears falling from her
eyes and the trembling of her lips. "Should I stop or continue?"
I asked myself. Should I take the time? I was in a hurry, looking
for the Savior. "Slow your pace. She is in trouble and needs
your help," the voice within me said. What could I do? So, with

regret I took the time. It was God's time anyway. I listened to the woman whose fate tugged at my heart. We talked for a while. What I had done or said I know not still.

Nonetheless, it eased her pain, and I was on my way. I was seeking the Savior, and there was nothing more to say. A lone cloud appeared above my head. The lightning struck. The sound of thunder was loud and fierce. Then the rain began to pour. There was great fear in my body; I felt helpless and all alone. But to me it mattered not, for I was seeking the Savior never to be alone. The lightning, the thunder—they quieted, and the rain began to end. With muddy feet and a glad heart I was on my way. There was a smile in my soul, and joy guided my feet. I was seeking the Savior, and here in this place I could not stay.

Then to my dismay but not surprise, I heard the drums of death marching our son and daughters off to war. The dread within me rose with such pain and sorrow, the level of which I had never known. Would they live or cease to exist? Here I was looking for the Savior, and our son and daughters were going off to war. I felt that for them I must be brave. I dried the tears from my eyes, but they continued down my face. I gently touched their cheeks, reminding them that the Savior was there marching with them off to wars. Some cried his name; others pondered the thought. I knew I had done my best. With a lighter heart and dusty feet I returned to my task.

Once more I was on my way. My mission was to seek the Savior, and that was what I must do. To my dismay I did not get far. Here before me were children; they joyously surrounded me. It was a wondrous and beautiful vision to behold. I watched their joyful play, and their pleasure filled me. There was much delight in their enchanted mood. We sang of men and the pleasures of the Savior and all he had done for us. As the years faded away, I watched the children go. Some became adults and grew older with the years. Others became memories and left me standing there. I smiled and relished the pleasure they had brought to all. I placed my hands upon my hips, for I had far to go, and I must continue on my way.

I had a calling I must fulfill. I was seeking the Savior, and I knew not how long I'd be. I knew I must stay the path, so I ambled on the way. I felt a warm and gentle touch. I looked to the skies. The light was so bright my eyes could not see. This must be the Savior I had sought. My body was light, and I felt as if I would take flight. "At last," I said. "He is here to take me home." This was the Savior that I had sought for so long. "Where are you off to, child?" I heard him clearly ask. "I am coming to meet you, and I did not want to be late," I replied. He held out his hand to me. I held my hand out for the Savior, and I knew it was him. These words he spoke to me: "My beloved, when your time here is done, there will be no need to look for me. I will come for you."

Love Is Action

Love is a verb, a word
that requires action.
Have you used the
actions of Love today?
Have you proved your
love for others lately?

Tomorrow is never
promised, except in the
deeds of yesterday.
Have you performed
some action that is more
powerful than words?
Someone I knew long
ago said, "Words are
just something someone
said." Truer words have
never been said. "I love
you" requires action, not
thought. Have you given
a hand up, or did you
stand on the sidelines
and voice your opinion?

What did you do to
prove your love for
others? Did you say to
someone who had lost
their way, "I love or I
care" and then leave
them there alone?
Walking on by would
have been more truthful
and have hurt less. It is
better not to lie to a soul
in need than to give a
promise in deceit. Have
you put your words to
action this day, or have
you given a promise and
then carelessly walked
away? What do you
think of you?

The Lessons of life

Life is full of maybes and
tomorrows. These two things
bring about "I should have" and
"I could have." Life is the living
and the doing. The doings
should be done today. Later

doings may never happen, for there is no promise of earth's tomorrow. The past is for remembering and learning. It can bring joy or sadness. The past is there now; it is forever a lesson that can be learned.

I or someone did this, and the results were wrong. The teaching of our past helps us to avoid disasters. We can use those lessons for today. All doings must begin in the now. Doing it now decreases the likelihood of "should," "what if," "maybe," or "could have." The lessons of life is to increase the "I did," "I learned," and "I have." Then there is the knowing that it all is true.

He Made Me Master

On the day of our births he said, "You are your master." What a quandary he gave us and wrapped it in a delightful dilemma. For how can I, a mere human, be master of a soul such as me? Why should he give such a prize to one who did not know the path, one who surely might give it away?

He knew some of our choices would cause harm, yet he did it anyway. He made us masters over all that was ours so that we could reign. He knew we would fall short, yet he gave to us the chance to have honor. Why did the Father make masters when he could have had slaves?

The gauntlet he threw down; choices he offered had to be made. We can pick it up or leave it alone. For then the choice will be made for us. No matter your actions, it is up to you, for no choice is also a choice. No human is a slave to the Father. How can he be made slave to the whims of man?

Remember Me

He stole my life, though it was not his to take. I was pushed in a car. He beat, robbed and lastly killed the one that was me. The stealing of my innocence and the beatings were ghastly crimes but taking my life was his final insult. After he filled my grave and placed the stone. He dusted his hands and wiped them upon his jeans. "That's it', he said. Foolishly he thought that was the end of me.

To him I was an insignificant thing to be discarded, thrown aside and forgotten I was less than the dog that he professed to love so dearly. He went about his days with seldom a thought of me. I was no longer a concern. I had served his purpose for I had briefly brought a measure of joy to his twisted mind. Now my life and even my death held no meaning for him. For in his thinking my dying was all of me.

When dreams of me invades his thoughts they were sharp bits of anger that my pain was no longer there. He felt no remorse or concern for the ones I had love and left behind. My child, my sisters, brothers and a man I loved dearly where on that list. In my release from life I made friends and touched lives. Even I did not know that in my dying would not be the end of me.

The new friends I made in death learned of my living as they cared for the ones I had known in my living. Though I am not with the living there is a part of me that still remains. The Father in his wisdom has built a world where I am its center.

That center is filled with more love and caring that ever before. The Master's love was my center. A life stolen could never be the end of me.

A Call to Meet My Father

Hello. [*laughter*] Why did you rush to the phone? I know, I do hate talking to machines. You need to stop. The way we love to talk we will be here all day. I know you are on your way to work. I thought you would be gone by now, Ms. Early Bird. Let me ask you this. I have a win-win request. You know me, I like win-win situations. I know. I love that about me too. [*laughter*] Why don't we just form a mutual admiration society? That's why we are friends. The thing is, I am calling because there is someone I would like you to meet. You better be teasing me. I would not be that insensitive. That's why I am calling. I have someone you must meet. We all need someone. He is the one person we all need in our lives.

Have you met my Father? Could I introduce him to you? Oh yeah, you'd like him. When can I come by? There is no need to leave where you are. My Father would be happy to come to you. Don't worry, he is my Father. He does this sort of thing all the time. He loves to help. Dear heart; that is my Father's way. He is like no one I have ever known. I have to tell you there is one catch, it is a good thing though. That is what make my Father so unusual. All He asks is that you serve others as he serves you. You are right; there are always rules. I'll tell you what. Oh! I would like for you to read the rules before we come, or we could read them with you. Okay, we can do that. It's not long. There are ten rules for living.

Let me tell you where to find them. Better yet, I will e-mail it to you. I could not have said it better. If my computer was a person, I'd be madly in love. You can read them, and I will call back tomorrow. So you can decided if you want us to come by or we can meet somewhere. Either way I will be in touch. You can call me between the hours of 8:00 a.m. and 8:00 p.m. But you can call my Father anytime. He doesn't care if it is day or night. Hey, on second thought, after you read, call him. Don't worry about the number. You will get it after you read the rules. I've got to go now. I want to make as many calls as I can. Don't forget, call me. Yes, we are still on for lunch next week. But telling you about my Father was something that could not wait. You could say that it is urgent. Bye, see you later. Love you. Click!

The Three

My body is tired, and my spirit seeks rest. They both have entered the realm of weary. The soul says in a commanding voice, "We are three. We are a body, a spirit, and a soul. We are all together. There are three of us as with the Savior." The soul says, "Hold on, for tomorrow will come." I know it is true but the doubt remains.

Maybe that day is a day in time that may or may not come. Tomorrow is a coming, just as today is here and it is now. Without the one, the others are only a thought in no one's mind. There is the Father; then there is the Son, and then there is the Holy Ghost. So shall it be with us. Doubt ends when the man, the body, and the spirit come together as a whole.

The Devil's Raid

The devil went out on a raid today. There was pain and much destruction.

It was an awful devilish display. Buildings shook. Sadly, we all share a loss.

His guise was complete and with nary a flaw. Oh, what a demon. Wily he was.

He was clever in his unique veil; the people were all made to appear the fools.

Was it those angelic eyes, or was it that wonderful childlike innocence he faked?

The specter with his cloak and a childlike smile completely duped us one and all.

He came to us as one we loved, to one whom we'd given much trust and our hearts.

The surprise was perfect, diabolically common; unknowingly all were deceived.

We danced with the devil and knew it not; what a shrewd fellow the devil was.

We listened not to the Father; and for this we lost our loved and cherished ones.

We were given a plan for his defeat but we ignored; the price of a raid is souls lost.

We prayed for pure sight and vision, for losing any soul is too high a price to be paid.

Father, we hear and will give obedience. The tools you gave we laid them far aside.

Now know we'll do our best to prevent a raid on the next and every other life-lived day.

Light and Dark

There is a place found between darkness and light.
It is the twilight before light of dawn or dark of night.
In this place are struggles and the asking of questions.
It will be settled. Will I live in the dark, or do I live in light?
The question and answers are decisions to be made by me.
Will I choose the light, or will I choose to live a life with dark?
Each answer is easy, but words from the lips of men are fickle.
Choices such as these have caused scores to die and nations to fall.
A home in the kingdom requires a good soul and strength of mind.

The side of darkness is false, and it will require nothing from you.
If you give yourself over to the dark, he will stomp that soul of yours.

Kneel Down, Spirit

Kneel down, spirit, and accept the word of the one Father.
Kneel down, spirit, and cleanse yourself with his living blood.
Elevate yourself; spread his words to them who know him not.

Elevate, spirit, and wash thy friends and foe with the holy book.
Walk spirit, as one of the living who has cast aside the damned.
Walk spirit, for you have requested, and God has accepted you.

Live in the spirit of the one who has purified you to make you whole.
Live in the spirit of the one who gives and cherishes as no one can.
Give spirit to the world as the Father has given unto all his valued flock.

Give spirit to those who cannot give; pray for the haves that they too give.

Spirit know that you are treasured by your creator as you treasure him.

Spirit, serving the Father has value none can know except the ones who serve.

So kneel down, spirit, and accept the crown of the one that saves our souls.

So kneel down, spirit; your name will be hailed and written in his book of life.

Kneel down, spirit; let it be said you have earned your seat, for the Savior is here.

Seeing with Human Eyes

I was off cruising for something good to do. There stood a man with unclean hair and grubby shoes. I turned my head to the side so him I could not see. Scum or criminal, I thought, it was obviously clear. How could someone of importance appear among men this way? I was sure he was of no importance, even though he smiled. I turned away and passed him by.

At the movie theater I saw a boy of eleven or so. He wore such dirty clothing. How could any mother allow her child to be seen this way? She must be on drugs. Maybe the child was too. My judgment was sound. I'd lived a lifetime, and I knew how these people were. They were always looking for a handout, never a hand up. They were lazy, slothful and dirty folk.

Tonight I awoke in a bed that was not my own. There stood a man who held a strong resemblance to the grubby man of the morning. "How did it go today, Doctor?" I heard the nurse ask. "Danny and I finished the mission. Doris called and said he was at the theater in the same dirty clothes." He laughed. "I could not be mad; he was there to save her life."

I closed tight my eyes. This now-clean man I did not want to see. I could lie to myself and make believe he was another. But God knew my thoughts about the man. He knew how I had felt about the boy and his mother. "God, forgive me for the fool I've been." I had seen life only with human eyes. Thank you, God. You sent an innocent child to save me.

Happy Valentine's Day

Roses can be red, violets can be blue,
But I have a problem, when you are that way too.
You are a dear friend, and I want only happiness for you.
Look around and see the love that is always there for you.
Love is one of those rare jewels that hide within the earth.
It is often in front of us. We do not see it, because we fail to dig.
You my love one was worth the effort to dig. Happy Valentine's Day!

I Thank God for Sending You

I have been to the mountain, and I have viewed the fruits of the
Promised Land.
In his wisdom he gave me a look at the promise he would soon
place in my life.
He knew I was fine on my own, but he knew
that I would be better with you beside me in
life. I bless him for bringing us together. Only
God could choose one for me as special as
you. I thank you, God, for sending her to love
me. To you, God, I say thank you for joining
us together in your eternal loving hands.

Darling, I Love the Way You Move Me.

Darling, I love you, and more I love the ways that you are moved.
You move me in the way you care for me and ones around you.
You move me when you come to me and place your hand in mine.
You move me when I look, knowing your lips will soon touch mine.
Darling, these are just a few of the things I feel when I look at you.

My love, I feel caring, tenderness, and passion, but there is more.
It is the way you love me with your all, and it must be love
returned.
Darling, "I love you" is not enough to give to someone such as you.

It is only a beginning for the love you give, is a love that never ends.
For all this and much more, darling, I love the way that you move me.

I Love You in Many Ways

I love the tenderness in your eyes when I smile at you.
I love the way my heart responds when our lips touch.
I love the way you know when things are not good for me.
I love the way you champion me in moments great and small.
I love the way you allow me to be me and make my own way.
I love the way we come together; when you and I becomes us.
Remember when we are old and gray, I love you in so many ways.

My Mother Placed Her Best in Me

Before I was born, I believed my mother did rejoice.
For me she did better, for me she did her best.
No mother can regret when she gives her finest.
The beginning in our world was God, her, and me.

Never Doubt That "I Love You"

I know "I love you" is just three small words.
They are casually said most every day. Heart
of my heart, you know me. Know that for me,
these three words will be a way of life, a vow,
a promise never to be broken. Never doubt
that I love you even if I sometimes forget to
say the words. To me these words hold great
value. When I say them to you, the look on
your face is worth more than all the riches
the world could ever know. And when you
say them to me, my world is made right.
Forever is too short a time to spend with one
such as you. So I'll ask God for one more
day for you and me. Heart of my heart, never
doubt that I love you!

No Christmas without God

There would be no Christmas without God. He gave his only son
so we may live. He gave to us the baby Jesus. What a wondrous
God he is. What an unending present he gave. It was such an

amazing gift. It was given to last forever. He gave it to me. He gave it to you. Today is the time. He said to ask and it would be given. How could I not love him for the gift? How could I not praise him in soul and spirit? God gave Jesus for all who want forever. That is you and me.

There would be no Christmas without my Jesus. No one more wonderful can be found. He offers us an incredible reward. He gave what no other could give; he gave himself and more. He was sent by the Father. He knew he would suffer and die to live again. Because of him we know the way. He offered love and life everlasting. What a present Jesus gave to us. Will you accept this most precious gift? What will you do, for there is truly no Christmas without Jesus who was given by God?

Come

Come, my friends, listen and hear. I have such a glorious tale to share. I have made reservations for a place over yonder. It is a place that will be made just for me. My ticket is my faith. Tending my garden is my work. Then there are choices I must make. Preparations are required if you wish to go there. I would enjoy a world of others on this journey with me. So join; come with me.

Where would you look to find answers? All instructions are there in the pages of your Bible. With faith and works, if you so choose, you can have one of your own. There are seeds to plant and a garden to be tended. The garden is all yours, so you must be rigid and stand firm against incoming weeds. Weeds, though small, can be demanding. The toil buys the ticket for your seat in heaven.

God and Me

In my life as a Christian, is it all about God and me?
I should pray for others with a zealous and kind heart.
I am to give to the ones in physical and spiritual need.
For maximum effect I must give with a happiness of spirit.
It matters not what others do; it is about God and what I do.
It behooves us to befriend the friendless ones who are without.
All these and more God has given as my fulfilling tasks of labor.
If my vineyard I do not tend; I am of no use to God or to others.
If I should not follow his instructions, he will not ask others why.
In his book of my life, it is not about others; it's my deeds for God

Not Looking

I was not looking for him, but God was looking for me.
My mother told me that God was with me always.
I was not looking for him, but he remained there.
My father says God will be there in my darkest hours.
I was not looking for God, but in his wisdom he was there.

I was not living in a place where I wanted God to be.
My grandmother said that all I had to do was believe.
I was not looking for him, but he remained there.
My grandfather said I could call on him at any time.
I was not looking for God, but in his wisdom he was there.

I was walking alone and foolish in the deeds I had done.
I sat in a restaurant with my friend, and there was God.
I turned a corner, not seeking anything, and he was there.
I went to the house of my loved ones, and there God was.
God knew my need and he was forever there ahead of me.

The Promises of Love

When I first saw you there was warmth in my soul, and then you turned to face me. I thought, *This is it.* I could define what it was. But I knew it was something I had never felt before. When you smile at me, I can't help but smile back. Now I know what that warmth was. It was the meeting of two souls, yours and mine. Saying "I love you" does not express the way my heart soars when we are together. But know for me, "I love you" is a way of life, a promise, and a vow never to be broken.

If I forget to say "I love you," know that the love is there. When I see you, know that you mean more than all the riches of the world. When you say "I love you," my world is made right. I love the way you care for others and me. Darling, you are wonderful. I feel that a lifetime is too short to spend with someone as special as you are. So I'll ask God for more.

A Child of Need

He was a babe of no importance to most of the people in the world. Standing there on the dirt floor of an old torn-down house, he could find no love at all. He looked to the darken skies and wondered how the world could be so cruel. What could he have done in his short life except to enter the world from his mother's womb?

His memories of her had begun to fade, for he was busy finding the necessities for survival in this worldly life. But what he remembered were her eyes of shame as she held him close in her arms. She had given him her life's blood, but for her child she had no food or comfort to give. He could feel the tears she cried as they fell upon his face.

And she said the last words he would hear her speak. "Darling, I must go. I am so sorry I have no gifts to leave for you." He held her close, even when she was cold, for her body was all that he had. He hid when they came to take her away. He knew not of goodness, empathy or kindness. His only love was her. Now she too was forever gone.

People of the world, while buying your new cars or some other treat you just must have, consider someone who needs you. Giving to someone who has needs instead of wants could be good for you. Could you—would you—think about a child or someone who cries out in pain because they have little or nothing, nothing at all?

The Cry

I heard her cry. Some said it was the cry of the damned. What would I know? I had not heard that cry before. I did not know what to do. I saw him as a sorry state of affairs; the agony was there within his eyes. What was I to do? I knew not; so for my sister and brother I prayed.

I thought prayer to be the cure of circumstances big and small. Now I know that it cannot cover it all. A prayer is just words someone said. A prayer is void without the power of faith. So I prayed but would not touch the flesh of my sister and brother's hands.

For the warmth of the touch was hard to bear. Prayer was my excuse for not doing. I could show God that there was love within my heart. Prayer is an excellent tool, but for me it was my way out. It was not my way out of the prayer but out of what I knew that I could do.

I could not allow it; the feeling of the touch would show the fear and it would stroll through my mind. Coward that I was, I prayed. The world would say my heart was pure, that I was shy with my feelings. What do they know? Words of the mouth are easy indeed. It is my greatest fear is that I will be touched by the world.

The Thing

Standing here looking at myself, I cannot see what lives inside of me. Maybe I can step outside myself to see what I can see. "What?" I cried. No! Not me. This is not me the one I wish to be. The sight my spirit doth see my mind cannot not comprehend or tell of. Nevertheless, it is my duty to tell of it. Though this was not me the one I wish to be. There are no words to describe the sight, but for others I must do my best. It is barely a body holding no form. It was ugly and filthy in the sight of God. This thing upon which I gazed—surely it could not be the person I thought I was. I pray my eyes are deceitful. God, will you help me? I wish not to be the thing I see. If this thing is me, it must go. It is not what God wants and wishes me to be. The thing has been dissected and evaluated. Why am I less than I was meant to be? I had a need to understand this thing I see. This Thing is not meant to be me. I had to figure out how to return to what I was before this thing became me. "No," I said to myself. I will not be the thing I see. I want to be what God wants of me. I will not be a wasted life. I will not be in a place where God does not approve of the Me I see. So I gather myself and do what I must. Children of the Father know there is work to do.

Are You Dying?

I heard the words. He said, "I am dying." Then there was a disillusioned voice that replied, "So are we all." The words were true, but so was the reply. Each day we all are living to die just a little to be reborn. For each and all it will come. It might be in a moment or many times over the years.

Death is a constant; it is bound to happen. But a death is a death, or so I've heard. Truth or not, it cannot be denied. It will come at night or during the day. Death can be slow or quick. These are matters left in the hands of God, so why should it matter that death is on its way?

Although death in itself is no guarantee for a joyous after, except for those who do the Father's best. Death is like the leaves of trees. We all have a season, but the leaves of man are not so clear. Death comes when it comes and takes its choice. Choose your death or not; it will be coming for you.

There are those who run to fight its light. Some seem destined to find only dark. Plans can be made by us or not. Death is not an expiration seen or made by man. True is true. Each soul will and shall be wrapped in the famous embrace of the one called death, be it one or many.

Make a Stand

I closed my eyes to the world, and I heard such a voice call out to me. I fell upon my knees, and he held out his arms. When I looked into the face, I knew that I was part of something greater than all the woes of the world.

He has placed me here to make my stand. He gave to me sisters to stand with. He gave to me brothers to walk with. And together with all, we will make our stand. And nothing can stop us as we make His stand.

I know that there is more for me. The purpose is now clear. Stand up. Hold out your hand. Place it in your Savior's hand. There is a task for me and for you. Take your place and stand up at the master's side.

Baby Girl

Today I was given a baby girl. I named her Melissa. The name means "honeybee" or "honey." Either will suit her best. As I look into her tiny face, I wonder who and what my baby will be. That is one left to God and her.

My prayer is that she is kind of spirit and clear in mind, body and heart. May she love intensely and live with much passion. Blessings for all she is and will do with her life. Fly, honey. Honeybee, fly. Mommy love you.

A Promise of Tomorrow

My body is tired; my spirit has begun to embrace the weariness in me. My soul says, "Hold on, there is a tomorrow. The Savior is on the way." The human is me just has to have its say. "Tomorrow is a day that never comes." I will not listen to the human, for He and I can make it understand.

My soul says to the human in a soft, commanding voice, "You are the body, and I am the soul. You are the one who can lead us astray. Do not forget that there are three of us, as there is the Savior. There is the Father, the Son, and the Holy Ghost."

"It takes all three, as it will with us. We are three, and together we win or lose. We have a body that houses a spirit, surrounds and encases a soul." The soul says to the human, "Without a tomorrow there is no today. Today is now. I accept a promise of Heaven's tomorrow."

Today I Have a Son

Today my life again changed. I became a mother to a child, my son. He is quite vocal. It is his voice I hear. Yelling and demanding though he may be, he is mine. He is God's gift to me. Come my son we have work to do.

He is beautiful, thin, and pale. It's not his fault, for my forefathers are the ones to be blamed. This is the way God sent him to me. And to him I must return my son. Without the Father I have no way of knowing what I am to do.

I have heard the old ones say a woman can raise a son but not a man. When I conversed with the Father, he set me straight. It is not a woman's place to raise a man. I am to raise a son to be a man, but God will make the man.

The Salt and the Seasons

You are the salt and the seasons of my world. You add flavor to all I do. You give hope in the presence of despair. You bring joy in the midst of sadness. You are the brilliance of the shining light.

You are the sweet smell in the stench of mortal death. You are a love for those who seek it but look in wrong places. You alone give mercy in a desolate world. Thank God he is here.

A Soul Lost

I had a friend who hungered, but I had no food to fill the need.

So, I visited with another and stole, for he was a man of plenty.

I had a friend who had no shoes, but I had none that I could give.

So I went to another friend and stole, she had no need and many.

There were children who had no clothes, but I had none I could give.

I received an invitation and stole; there was much; so none to be missed.

They gave awards and accolades for all that I had done, deserved or not.

When the Father called, I searched for my soul; sadly I'd none I gave it away.

Granny and Us

As I look back over the world of my life, I see and I remember my grandmother's love. She was a mother and a grandmother too. She gave to us all the love that she had. And she somehow seemed to find more. She was a bit more than three feet tall.

How could one so small carry such an overflowing of love inside?
Where was the love, and where did it hide? When we were not
sure if she could love us more, she, in turn, gave even more.

The Road to Oneness

We know in your hands of love an eternal future will come where
we all will be one. There is a place between darkness and light; it
is the twilight between dawn and night. In this place there is a
struggle and a question to be settled. Will I live in darkness or
choose light? The question has two answers: I will live as God
has commanded, or I will stand within the dark.

Each answer is easy. Thought words from the lips of men are
often fickle. They cause men to die and nations to fall. A home
in the kingdom requires much mastery of mind and faith of
spirit. It ask the same of the physical body. The darkness
requires nothing of you, just that you allow yourself to be
pulled into a tide of ruin. It is your want and your choice! Will it
be oneness with God or the Devil and Hell.

See Me

"Mom, today the others made fun of me and laughed out loud,"
said the child to the mother. "Mom, what is wrong with me?"
"Darling, you are perfect in every way," said the mother to the

child. "God made us as different as he did alike. So be glad of it. God love you; rejoice in your difference". Unsure the child sought out her father.

"Daddy, they said I was ugly. My eyes are too big, and my nose is not like the others," said the child to the father. "Daddy, what is wrong with me?" "My beloved child, you are as God made you. In man's eyes, perfect things are imperfect, God sees the beauty in you." He loves and cares for you so don't despair.

That night the child knelt down to pray. "God; my mother said we should rejoice in our differences. Father said that you could see the beauty in me. God, I have a request. I need your help. Could you let others see what you, Mommy, and Daddy see in me? And, God, could you do it by tomorrow? Amen."

Words of Wisdom

Saying VI:
It is required of man that he always pray and never lose heart (Luke 18:1).

Saying VII:
Life is a series of events; what we do with those events shapes our future however long it may be.

Saying VIII:

Our destiny does not depend on who we know on the earth. Our destiny lies in the after living.

Mothers of the World

My eye doth see all my mothers of the ages and what they are to me. Their lives are here and in lands there. Some, abroad and outside my shores in corners I have not seen. They are underground and above. They are in caves, castles, and palaces of stone and gold. There are those in chains, cages, and cargo holes, crossing over lands and waters deep. They are many shades of women these mothers of the world. It matters not her color but that she is a mother.

There are those who adorn themselves in luxurious clothing of gold and jewels that none can equal. There are those in silk gowns and pearls; some are adorned in dresses of calico frayed from the use. There were those who wore what Mother Nature gave, beads of bark and hides made soft with chewing and from wear. These are many and long generations of my heritage and yours. No matter their skin texture; they are all me and you or some part thereof.

Each one worships and prayed to the One. They knew that they would prosper and find a way. I cannot say they knew they were praying for the future or if they prayed for their kin and me. They worked fields and cooked meals. They work in plants and offices, where work was found. They did what they could, as I must do. I am the mother of a generation praying for a future. I know not when, but I know it will come. So we all pray for the generations of worlds to come."

God, hold the hands of the mothers now and the future mothers who are yet not born. They are sending their children off in wars to defend their beliefs and ways of life. Mothers pray for their children and their children's children. It is a mother's calling. What else can the mother of a mother do? "God, hold the hands of the mothers now and mothers in the future that is yet to come." We know in your hands of love an eternal future will come where we will be as one.

Thinking of Me

Today I woke, and the world was dark and foggy.
But it was such a treat to awake from my sleep.
It would not happen except for the grace of God.
I thank you, Father, for thinking of little ole me.

Tomorrow the sun may be out; it could be bright.
Still, it will be such a treat to awake from my sleep.

It would not happen except for God's loving grace.
So I thank you, Father, for thinking of little ole me.

No matter the situation or its circumstances.
It will be such a treat to awake from my sleep.
It would not happen except for God's loving mercy.
So I thank you, Father, for thinking of little ole me.

Is He Dead?

God is not here. He is dead—at least that is what unsaved
people say.
They saw him hanging there, torn and bloody; on his head
thorns lay.
You should have seen the spears as they poked and pierced in
his side.
He's dead. They say, "What man could take such abuse and still
live?"
He hung his head, closed his eyes; and not another word was
heard.
When he was taken down, we all knew that his body was held in
a death.
What more proof do you need? Why do you stand and say he is
not dead?

God is alive in the saints, they say, for I feel him on the inside and outside too.

His body died to live again; he died and rose from the grave so I too may live.

He did not have to die, but he did it for me. Who could love me as much as he?

I close my eyes, and I know he is there; the world offers its own truth of the deed.

They praise from heaven and earth; there is joy in knowing He is alive and here.

What can I say? That is the way of God, to teach us a lesson of life after death?

Now the lesson has been taught. Did you learn? Faith is the key; Jesus is the door.

Content with God

Hear me, I have something to say. This is my life. Don't pity me. No sadness or pity is required. What we need is understanding and love for whom and what we are. We are his progeny, and he is our God. We must grasp and hold strong to the Father's hand.

You say to the other you are sorry for your illness and the things that you have lost. Then you say that you will pray. Did you? You should know that, with God, nothing of value is ever lost. God's children gain what others think of as lost and even more.

There is one who knows us better than we could ever know ourselves. He placed us where we are; we choose if it is good or bad. He does this so we may be prepared for what he is to give us. As his children, we are to do the task our Father has for us.

Know that if there is an obstacle, we must endure, and together with him we will overcome. If he allows one way to be blocked, know that another is opened. A closing window lets us see the door. Have the wisdom to know that even closed door is not the end.

When we walk in faith, we know that man's restrictions are God's possibilities—be it illness, disease, or afflictions of our own making. We have security in the arms of our Father. Because we are his own, he cares for us all. Serving him gives us security.

Sometimes we cannot hear, because we live as the world. But when we give him our attention, we find He may have answered the prayer but we saw it not. With him things are not always easy. It is not easy with the devil either, but the rewards with God are much greater.

What he wants of you, I do not know. Each of us has our own journey's end. Each must seek for themselves. Some will go with God; others will not. For me, I am his child and he is my father, so my path is with him. I can only be content if I am walking with God. But is he content with me?

Peggy S. McDougald

He Is Here

I lay down with God's loving grace, and I sleep.
He allows my eyes to open at the dawn of each day.
There is a miracle in the changing of the heavens.
It is there I feel his love and peace surround me.
I know I have nothing to fear, for my God is here.

I lay down at the end with God's loving grace as I sleep.
My eyes again open to the dawn of the day.
There is a miracle in the changing of the heavens.
It is there I feel his love and peace surround me.
I know I have nothing to fear, for my God is here.

I see him in the trees, every blade of grass he made.
I see him in the mountains, where he created every peak.
I see him in the waters, from the creeks to the oceans wide.
I see him in the heavens; different skies are colored everywhere.
I see it, and I know it is there, because God said it and it is so.

Me Again

It's me. I know you
told me to go away and you would take
care for me.
You said that you were here
and I had no need to be on
my own.
I have studied, and I can take
care and stand upon feet that
are my own.
You said we are brothers and
sisters; you said we should
stick together.
You said what was yours was
mine and mine yours. Tell me
now, is that true?

Friend, I have been with you
through thick and thin; I came
when you called for me. Now
it is my turn. All I ask of you is
that you give to me what I've
given to you. Before you said
I was not ready, that I need to
be qualified. So I did what you
said because it seemed right
to do so. My friend, here I am.
As you can see, it is me
again. I have come to claim a

portion of what you promised
to me.

If you remembered not, there
is a contract that you gave. I
ask less of you than I gave.
For me it was a labor of love;
on this I stake my claim.
Again you say, "Wait." Is
there something that I did not
know? Tell me what is wrong.
I have abided by the rules. I
have received degrees in
universities and colleges. But
I learned more lessons in the
world and the school of hard
knocks.

Could it not be me but the
way I look—my eyes, my
teeth, my feet, or my mind?
Friend, I have received
approval from the One on
high. With receipt of his
blessing for us there is no
more to say. Hear my words.
We will stand and take our
places. God's gift we will not
waste. I will not step aside,
nor will I go quietly away. The

Father sent me, and I am
here to stay. Friend, it is me
again.

My Foundation

It is me. I have words I am bound to say. This is my life. Look at me.
What I need is not sadness but understanding—for you, not me.
I am his progeny, and he is God; I will hold strong to my
Father's hand.
You say to me, you are sorry for my illness, are you.

There is nothing of value I have lost, and I have gained more each day.

I am his progeny, and he has given me all; I'll hold onto the Savior's hand.

There is one who loves and knows me better than I ever knew myself.
He places me where I am, so I can prepare and do the things I should.
I am his progeny, and I must go about doing the task he has for me.

I know if there is an obstacle, I must fight. I will try hard to overcome.
God said if one way is blocked, there is another direction in which to go.
Because I am his progeny, I shall hold strong to my Father's hand.

In life I have learned man's restrictions might be God's possibilities.
So bring on the wheelchairs, disease, and other afflictions of man.
I am his progeny, and I shall grasp strong upon my Savior's hand.

Sometimes he cannot talk to me, because I am watching the world.

But when God gets my attention, he gives me such wondrous gifts.
So there is no fear. I am his progeny, and I will hold strong to his hand.

What he wants for you I do not know. Each one has their own walk with God.
Together, God and I go about our task. He is with me, and I am with him.
He is the Father, and I am the child; for me, my foundation is with God.

Burdens

When my burdens of life are much too hard to bear, and I face a world of highs and lows,
There is a state where I can go. It is not a place of physical existence but an employ of mind.
The place in which I go can come in many locales. It could be the simple smile of a child. Or it could be the touch of a tender hand. It could be the breeze rustling in a tree or the cool misty swell of an ocean blue.

The earth is a balm for our burdens high and low. It is alive this earth of ours. It is living just as much as you or I. It lives and dies. It tears itself apart, changes, and then rebuilds. He gave it to us. This place we call the earth was once known as our Eden. Now it is a place of fifth and ruin. But the earth we call home will heal in time. For man and the earth I pray that the healing is not too late.

The Time

Today I took the time. I snuggled myself in my chaise under the shade of an old oak tree. I lay still and listen quietly to the world around and the world within the body in which I live. As I sit and let go of the world of man, I let the world of man pass me by. My troubles drift on the back of the wind.

I smiled as the birds sang a lively tune. The leaves joined in and sang a buoyant refrain.

The sound was sweet as it danced among the limbs of time. The wind greeted it and added to the music of the day. Below, the grass danced and swayed along. It was music that no one could deny. It was sheer joy.

The animals of the woods decided to join the choir. I knew not who they were, but it was filled with delight. Who would have thought that the animals could carry out such an affectionate response? It was a sound I did so dearly love to hear. Thank you, Father, for the quiet. I am blessed from a man-made day.

Is There Room?

I heard her say, "Will there be room?" As the words touched my mind, I knew it was not heaven of which she spoke. For in my Father's home there is room for all of those who seek his counsel and do his will. If you are one who changes your mind most every day, there are things you can do. Stop! Hanging to the left and then hanging right is not what your Father wants from you. What yours is yours though at times it will change. You must be willing transform yourself.

There is room in the kingdom of heaven for the committed and the ones with a faithful heart. Be not afraid, for the Father knows you well. He is aware of your soul inside and out. He knows you are human and sometimes you will stumble. If you ask of him, he will help you to bear the fall. It does not matter if your crisis is small or big. The Father is there for us all. If someone ask, "is there room"? Remember these words I have said to you. The Father has a place for each and all of his flock.

Words of wisdoms

Saying VIIII:
You shall love all your brothers as you would love yourself. Love them in and out of season, for they are the children of the Father.

Saying X:

Life is a gift of many treasures. Some are in sight, but do not find the ones of value because we fail to look.

A Toy

Although her heart was sad, she was filled with love, for this day a friend she had made. Her friend next door happily said, "I have a toy I do not want or need anymore." Sad but safely she sat on her floor; she was in a home with a grandmother she barely knew. As she was playing with the toy of a friend that was now hers, she was happy, for she had made a friend today.

There in the silence came a knock. The woman, her grandmother, hair filled with gray, opened the door. A man stood there, one she knew by sight, though he too had never spoken to her. It was the father of the friend who had given the toy he did not want or need anymore. There stood the man, angry and proud because of the toy the son had given away.

He looked at the child there. She played with the toy his hard-earned money had bought. He looked at her grandmother with a frustrated air. With a barely controlled voice, he demanded that the woman produce her son so that they could speak. The man looked around the room and heard from her throat the saddest of sounds. Before he looked back, the light of the candles caught his eyes. Pretty though the lights were, he knew it was because they had not lights.

Looking back at the woman he saw tears in her eyes, she said, "My son died last night from damage he suffered when your son and his friends robbed his store. But we hold no grudge," she quickly said. He shamefully apologized and wished her luck. As he crossed over her yard, he looked at the street and there the sign read, "Foreclose sale." He thought of his older son and of the younger one. One was a taker, the other a giver. The one who took was more like him.

He had placed aside the thought of the older son. He had gotten a lawyer. He never asked who his victims were. His son of twelve had known the child and likely knew the cause of their pain. His son had given something of value, a toy he prized. The man heard clearly the words of his son: "I have you. She has no one." For his son had him; a father. The man entered his home, embraced his son, and held on tight. He saw his son's heart. He gave his son a toy, but the child gave more.

Words of Wisdom

Saying XI:

He who gives money is much appreciated but he who gives of himself gives a gift that has infinite value; they give a piece themselves.

Saying XII:

God place such value on us that he gave his son. This gives proof that one who does not value another places no value on himself.